When the Earth Flies into the Sun

DEREK MONG

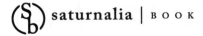

Distributed by Independent Publishers Group
Chicago

©2024 Derek Mong

No part of this book may be used or reproduced in any manner without written permission except in the case of brief quotations embodied in critical articles and reviews. Please direct inquiries to:

Saturnalia Books
2816 North Kent Rd.
Broomall, PA 19008
info@saturnaliabooks.com

ISBN: 978-1-947817-72-2 (print), 978-1-947817-73-9 (ebook)
Library of Congress Control Number: 2024935289

Book design by Robin Vuchnich

Cover Image: Francis Bacon, *Three Studies of Lucian Freud*, oil on canvas, 1969, triptych, each panel 198 x 147.5 cm (CR no. 69-07), private collection. © The Estate of Francis Bacon. All rights reserved, DACS/Artimage 2024. Photo: Prudence Cuming Associates Ltd

Distributed by:
Independent Publishing Group
814 N. Franklin St.
Chicago, IL 60610
800-888-4741

CONTENTS

"When the Earth Flies into the Sun	3
Partially Restored Statue of a Silver Bull	6
The Ghost Ship	8
To a Future Mass Shooter	9
How to Keep Yourself Awake	11
The Reality Television Star	12
Ode to the Elephant's Foot	14
The Journal of Glacial Archaeology	16
A Poem for the 21st Century	19
To the First Speaker	21

❧

A Poem for the Scoundrel Lucian Freud	26
Odes to Asklepios	37
Midnight Arrhythmia	43

❧

For the Gods Now Gathering Over Omaha, Nebraska	55
The Fog at Leadbetter Point State Park	57
Gegenschein	59
The Cloud	62

Exhausted Renegade Elephant	63
In the Land Between Sex and Conception	65
The Dead Cooper's Hawk	66
Ode to Aphaea	68
For the Last Human	70

The Period at the End of This Sentence	73
NOTES	77

for Annie

and for Whit

"When the Earth Flies into the Sun

it will be morning every day,"

    a dawn of lost receipts & dial tones,

     of unpaired socks surviving last night's wash—

  we'll slip one on and step   into our liquefying windows.

 We'll shake the burrs

  fastened to our ribcage: resentments our lovely, hungry-

    for-attention kids have spurred; the guilt these resentments

engender—

   all will have gone to glare.   Let us bless this blindness

    we saw coming.

Even animals (extinction's avant-garde) recognize   this freedom—

  terns flee the timberline's flame;

     the fox's frustrated lusts

         immolate within him.

 And we who burned so much   before we burned—

is this our balm for that truth   we too gradually

conceded: *the earth is ours to alter.*

My ambition dissipates like fog

till the world leaves me (briefly,   if completely)

      with nothing more   to lack, no one to compare to.

So let us float

      through interstellar motes of dust,

  until another species gleans us   from our least hurtful refuse:

the space shuttle's bolts,   an astronaut's discarded napkins.

This is how   the six-year-old son

      of our dear friends

    imagined our future alien meeting. He was stargazing

                    in an open field when he turned

                      to me and gave this poem its first sentence.

Partially Restored Statue of a Silver Bull

Delphi – sixth century BCE

Like cattle shrapnelled   or beef tips in tinfoil

you don't cohere   into a steer

                                                  till our eyes (blink, blink) rebuild you.

        Haunches, hooves   hung in air—

        what wine pairs   with the Platonic ideal   of idol?

❧

Read the plaque; snap a picture.

Some dude made you—   another dude prayed

                                            and paid   for you

           to flare your nostrils   flick a mylared ear.

        (Fleshy blessing!   Worship to make   a good impression!)

Briefly famous on the Sacred Way,

your owner's face   wobbled on your flanks—   you were expensive thanks.

❧

Then dispersed, despoiled,

                you'd rise

                              like a ghoulish prize   through centuries & soil—

to teach us—   what?

That archaeology's part luck?   Part art?   All toil?

                                ❦

Dose us   with shimmering hypnosis—

Reprise   that old lie: our ancestors

                                      were smarter *and* more industrious.

Or just bear us—like the passers-by   who smudged

                           your hide—   nearer to Olympus.

                                ❦

We pass you   and pass through

                              an oracular thought of bull—

                                        your glass case: Apollo's skull—

                                        his synapses sparkle   piecemeal.

          I'll leave you

                incomplete   and ethereal.

The Ghost Ship

The sea surrounding them they barely knew;
the fog was constant. Sirens trailed the violence
through the hills but taught them silence.
Their son would learn to walk along these avenues.
Date night downtown: they slipped into a fugue
of cocktailed youth they hoped to hold against
the rising tide of parenthood, the rents.
They parked a car where once there'd just been dunes.
Earthquakes whispered up their trees.
They read of ships left crewless in the harbor
whose wreckage stretched the nation's western bounds.
Once their child ran heedless into the sea.
Their front porch shrugged and split its mortar.
Occasionally they dreamt the other drowned.

To a Future Mass Shooter

If I could touch you

I'd touch you   where your wrist meets your hand.

       Your tendon relaxes   like grass bending to the sand.

    Set down your duffel.

    Let it grow into a dune.

         The shoreline here flashes   like a faded cartoon.

Do your victims complete you   like family   or a creed?

Do their names   fill your evenings

                       like the hum of cable TV?

Tell me yours.   I'll write it down here

           if that would just end it.

             I've few readers, but they're kinder   than Reddit.

You must know   that you haunt us already.

Can you see   our deaths

           predate you?   (They're like waves—distant, but steady.)

    Our children rise up   in their swings

           and never come down.

    Our screen doors swing open—   *no one's home, no one's home.*

❧

Light me a cigarette; pour me a shot.

Let us do—at this driftwood table—what   your dark tools cannot.

    The sun

        will soon tan us back into ash—

           why not raise a glass   to our bodies' slow rot?

How to Keep Yourself Awake

Think of the kiddo

when his doctors botched

limbs ungainly,

swept into siloes

Now picture his parents—

learning to love

How do you weigh

against his gliding

And what'll they share—

save this awareness:

in peaceable rhythms

cursed to the chasm

one drug's dose:

sight & hearing

swollen with thought.

pain-vexed, voided—

by wordless touch.

the wails they wade through

toward gulfs unknown?

his sweet-sense savaged—

daylight will rally

the plants all know.

The Reality Television Star

My days are lit like Emmy statuettes.

I only glow because I'm envied.

                Were you taught that screens fossilize our thoughts—

as if in amber a word (once heard) was sealed?

        Do you think me mutable   like cable news?

I am duller than I let on.

I improvise a life to lift your own,

           using my time with *him* or *her*—my so-called fellow stars—

to nest inside your ear.

    The ouroboros of self-regard,   I view myself everywhere.

Watch me watch you

        from posters over subway cars.

    You check your cell phone's bars.   We're equals—or so the network feels—

        in our need for love

    and listeners.

Does acting help you   meet friends who seem free?

Do you go home as bored as me?

        I aspire to pyrrhic fire

        but found myself—

                swipe right, swipe left—persisting under fingertips.

I've learned the joys of direct address:

    I am yours.

    I can still be hers or his.

        In this I mimic public speakers   (pols or preachers)

    recharged by the enfilade of flashbulbs.

        I am smaller than I once appeared

but return, tiresome as spring.   One day you'll vote me your new king.

Ode to the Elephant's Foot

Reactor Number Four

*   *   *

*   *   *

*   *   *

Nuclear loogie – irradiated
slurry – lumps
of lava that boogied

floor by floor – freed
from a collapsing core –
you are – *what?*

Hubris as a molten heap
of shit – a scald
on Sisyphus's fingertips?

You'll still kill
ten thousand years from now –
so lethal

only words
can come near you
(two pics exists – click, split)

May the eons remake
you : time capsule
to prove we all were assholes –

Gibraltar for post-
apocalyptic others – or relic
to rally faith's fanatics

You mimic
your namesake –
hulkingly fatal – memory's

mute receptacle –
but nest instead inside
a mess that nests

in a Soviet sarcophagus –
tumor that nurtures
a thesis

from a rumor:
it's our mistakes
that will outlive us

* * *

* * *

* * *

The Journal of Glacial Archaeology

1.

Baskets, brooms, & arrowheads
        with "lashings perfectly preserved";
                the dregs from jugs

        that tell how Incan youths
got drunk; and then a field
                of fetid reptiles the cold

                no longer deigns to hold—
its scent alerts a lucky
researcher who runs

to beat the baking sun.
        "For every discovery," this editor
                concedes, "there are

        thousands decomposing."
Bodies, he means, the relics
                hardest to recover.

                There is, we learn, so much
        left to learn. His boon
is good if misbegotten.

2.

Mount Hood in early spring:
    its southern face a glaze
        the sunlight sloughs away.

    Blots of dirt break through;
the dirt—it's dark—absorbs
        the light, the light is hot

    and heats the earth—
    the earth thaws a thinning snowpack.
The melt will spread like melanoma.

And yet there's snow enough
    for us to rent inner tubes
        we roll uphill

    then race down together.
Look at us, my love: a family
        that moves in one direction.

        That is until our son
    insists on sailing solo.
Lawyerly, dwarfed at five

by this tire's insides,
    he says he wants
        to learn his limits.

    Let him make mistakes,
the books all say.
        Mistakes are instructive.

3.

Hike past a heap of rocks that jut
        like dragon teeth and through
                a field concealed

        beyond the fir trees;
pass snowbanks like thick meringue
                and pause beside the pooling sunlight.

            Two figures are emerging.
        They rise as snow dissolves
in gauzy shreds, a sheet

drawn back to show fingers,
        heels, a leathery earlobe.
                By noon they breach the air:

        a small body wrapped
inside a large one. This is an age
                of deliquesced resurrection.

            This is love so pure—
        see how she turns his head, small eyes
buried in her breast—

that when catastrophe
        loomed, she held one thought:
                I cannot let him know it.

A Poem for the 21st Century

When the men in dark suits
blow a kiss to the mirror
and the bus driver imagines
his last rider as a souvenir;
when the skies crystallize
with the fire of crescendoing jets
and the phone shakes the table
and the table wobbles
to the tune of its shortest leg;
when newspapers gather
on doorsteps like neighborhood
strays; when all the scales
are uneven, and the butcher
retreats into the meat locker's haze;
when the wishing well dries
into a silt of spilled coin;
and the dinner plate slips
from your hand like a rind;
when the radio's static
is the last broadcast you can bear,
you walk to the shore
where time seems to stall
and track the erosion
that thinned the red bluffs
last fall. The surf tugs
at heels you've dug in the sand
and the sand fleas erupt
like an out of tune band.

The golf course is lit in the spot
where they bulldozed a lake.
You hear the sprinklers spurt on.
The patrons are all eating steak

To the First Speaker

You—who are kin to all clans;

You—who called the rain   we've been drowning in for eons;

    did you flinch to find   a shard of self

                                           split off—a passing thought

        unhidden?   Did it feel forbidden?

Or was it like the stone   you raised

       between your hands, and—gauging   its weight against your son's—

    tossed it   into a river?

                  Are we the mist   upon your arms?

                           Why do I assume you're female?

Your friends will look   away;

your dog will look and sniff   and walk—one paw

    unstuck from mud—into a clearing   you're on the cusp of naming.

       They will return.

                 They're new   to this brand of shaming.

And listening grows   more slowly

still—like a snowbank　　　　　　in the evening—

　　　as crowds form in twos or tens

　　　　　　　　　　to coin a word　　　that'll pass like a dark glance

　　　　　　　　　　　　　　　　　　　through a wake or wedding.

A Poem for the Scoundrel Lucian Freud

after Francis Bacon's 1969 triptych of the man

"Great British painters, one might say, imitate the proverbial behaviour of buses. None come along for a century or more, then two at the same time."

-Martin Gayford

1.

Stendahl's disease, I know, is bunk.

The spinning room & swoon, the paint—even Bacon's, all carnival

     grotesquerie—a psychic drain?   In truth, our blood sugar's low

       from oohing straight through lunchtime.

  And yet, I'm only steady at this bench.

 I see Freud's face travel like a triple stab; I see my love

     (wet viscera, lamp glare, O.R.) meet our son—

 and feel like one of Bacon's hundred butchered

2.

portraits.

  Lucian, Old Bean: it's February on the South Park Blocks—

  kids ride scoot bikes, the homeless sunlit—but you

     melt indoors, a body poured

into wicker chair & headboard,

    references, our curator claims,

   to your fourteen (acknowledged) children. My son's nearly four.

    We've stopped to see   the world's priciest portrait.

3.

And we, like you, are also three:

        my wife holds   our son's small hand; her free one finds, then slips

    inside, my fingers—   another under-the-kid's-radar

           communique   that's become our second nature:

                  He really needs to get outside   she means

                              but leans in & whispers: *Do you wanna keep looking?*

                  I do, my love, I do

   though your departure   leaves me outnumbered

4.

   and numb here, induced

           by Lucian's scoundrel charm—   disarming still from these canvases' hereafter.

   Why does the repulsive draw me closer?

                      Enviable talent, absent parent, he made

                                sex & paint his life's pursuits, eager

  to seed his world   with likeness.

Even now, bound in Bacon's gaze, he's fidgety & refracted—   beguiling

           as a volcanic plume encircling the planet.

5.

That planet turns   indifferent to the years

      it shears from our lifetimes. It turns, spurring us   toward self-making.

    We rake up whatever coals might glow

          beyond our starless nightfall—

   therefore children, therefore painting.

   My son pauses   beneath an exit sign; my wife glances

     at a landscape. What will follow is an hour, love,   parenthetical

   inside our parenting.   Kids are the afterlife that cost us all the others.

6.

Summer, 1982:   Lucian, you're dancing nude to Blondie's "Sunday Girl."

    A lover knocks, a would-be model.   You drink, you paint, you fuck—

       until the cassette tape stops   half-played, a moment unindulgent.

         Did you think to offer breakfast?

    And what *of* the woman who flipped through canvases   while you pissed,

       who found someone else's breasts, luminously hid?

Did she seek—like you, like me—maximum

            fulfillment? Did she turn up Deborah Harry?

7.

A decade later: Kate Moss lets you paint her.

She's often late "in the way that girls" are late (eighteen

minutes, you say), but still you'll fill a canvas *and* tattoo her—

little birds where future lovers pass,

your needle flitting in and over skin while you share a taxi.

Did the portrait distill you more? More blood

within its bounds— more *you* below its surface?

Your child, Annie: your first full-length nude; your Bella got Moss to model.

8.

First daughter born in '48, last son in '84,

upwards of 30 (unacknowledged) more absorbed—like rain

on English country roads—into their mothers' families.

Lucian, your lust enamors me

but less than this question: how did you ignore

the tradeoff that plagues me— being an artist *vs.* becoming a parent?

I picture women, men—sunlit, kids in hand—walking

into a gallery. One looks unwittingly at her father.

9.

World where *oughts*   like rural radio

        exhaust, passing as one passes from their signal's strobing   ambit;

    world of easements, world where meaning

                slips free of some biologically

    cold bond; world so new it flows—like you, Lucian—from the Old;

world where the gene pool is a canvas.   "How shall we make love tonight?"

        my new favorite character asks in the novel   (my wife sleeps;

    I read) about sex   in a French village.

10.

Your answer: with arrogant abandon.

You double-dipped into the self   you could endow, flecked

    paint like a post-coital trail,

                so beautiful, so boldly unrepentant.

Bacon was right to mangle you,   though few today take notice.

    I am the riverstone these visitors course round—

        the CCTV cams won't see me till they fast forward.   A ghostly flow

divides us then—   imagine your children *are* that blur;   imagine them inattentive.

11.

Some nights we threw the covers down.

Some nights we sought

                that lower ground where we dissolved coolly.

    This was years ago, our child's face a glaze   we separately imagined

then worked to make through sex (no work)   as you, Old Bean, had always

              understood it: limbic, unprotected.

    I stare into the faces Bacon lathed

                            and see the wound our love   created—

12.

red of rare steak, gray like smudged lace—

                could I unsee my love's C-section?

She was there and she was not there.

        I couldn't look and then I had to: the scalpel's soundless glint went in

    to find our child writhing   out from an incision.

And then a wail, two hands in air—

       he grasps at fur we haven't grown for ages.

    A Moro reflex, the nurse confirms: our first fear is falling.

13.

  A man will spend nine months   imagining a son

  until that son becomes a would-be poem: a name afloat, a nascent obligation.

He speaks to it but fails to see

    that his addressee is just his echo.

  I was goddamn Narcissus at the pond.

  I am still someone who talks to paintings.

Did you, Lucian, give a thought   to what your fucking

  wrought?   Did you grasp the casualties of imagination?

14.

And the surgeon put his staples in.

And my newborn squirmed, nuzzling my useless nipples.

  I imagined

    how he was our stone, a child who—for an hour now & hours

    more—we'd carry in tandem.   My wife nurses, I read; switch, repeat—

  our sleep & light & limb   indefinitely borrowed.

This painting, Lucian, returns me to

    useless fantasy: there were years I lived, like you, unburdened.

15.

Insomnia, a summer: siblings ghost across our bedroom floor.

They mountaineer our shelves

                      and nudge books onto the carpet.

    They commandeer the ceiling fan or build   fires inside our boxsprings.

We'd stopped at one

and he knew why before the lies we told him.

        "Will I have a brother soon?"   he'd ask, and, before I could reply—

        "Papa, when you die, I want   to hear your songs on the radio."

16.

My reply? ("Me too.")   All wrong.

I should have said:

          "Love—   most never have the chance to make them."

    Can you be haunted, Lucian, by kids   you did not claim?

I'm haunted by those I have denied him.

        Once you wrote: "The effects [that people] make on space"   will differ

    as "a candle and a lightbulb."

        But what of the glow absence holds—   our filament is cooling.

17.

I would, Old Bean—had I not (for years) asked   art & books to pinch-hit

       for God; were the consequences less certain—slash

               your triple face and slip my head   into each canvas.

     But let's be honest:

I am (white, well-off) leisured enough to lose   an hour to paint;

I am (a dude) fixated on a wound I have no claim to.

        So let me stand—

while half the city makes evening plans   and half prepares to serve them.

18.

There's a moment before you greet your child,

before they mark you as their own,

before they rise from all their little hands have done   and run toward you—

     before they're yours, you're theirs

and will be always.

      There's a moment before your spouse   recognizes the footsteps as your own,

       before she turns her head to break the fast   that is parenting solo.

         There's a moment when your family is a photograph

19.

        you could just walk away from.

My wife and son play hide & seek.   He peeks out

            from a pedestal—giggles give his place away—

  and she pretends

               she cannot see him.   There is so much to write

  about this scene—   how pigeons shake the trees,

               how an opera leaks from an upstairs window—

      if I just had time to.   A decade will fill with days like these

20.

and we'll pay handsomely to live them.

      And soon this game will end   in tiredness or squeals, cheeks

      smeared with applesauce, and napping

              on a bus that strums a bridge that steelworkers willed across a river.

For now, though, I loiter here—

      delaying the hours bound   for bedtime's diminuendo.

         I claim a spot beyond my wife's gaze,   past the kiddo's keener earshot—

              I see you, loves. I see you.

Odes to Asklepios

* * *

* * *

* * *

Bas-relief beefcake
— bare-chested, pecs *vexing* —
do staff & snake

protect us?
(My insurance card
sends its regards)

Epidauros jars us
— the bizzarest of exhibits —
breasts, cocks, arms

an array of clay
appendages
murmur: *where does it hurt?*

* * *

Take heart,
take cyst, take his wrist,
(my kid's in a splint)

take C's system nervous;
take my love's
lumbars plundered

of cartilage
and bulk up her bones
(osteopenic prongs)

so she and I can dive
– a compost synchronized –
through dirt,

decades, & earth – so we
can skeletonize
in tandem

*   *   *

Can we waterfall
our fingers
down this ancient lingo

– its rows like code –
to feel (or feel *for*)
those who came to heal?

Does this slab of gray
pray or say
what tools or tomfoolery

– what's a *thymele*? –
your priests
used here?

* * *

You – struck
dead for raising the dead –
You – rocketed

by divine light socket –
forgot the gods
cannot be Xeroxed

Want revenge?
Delay *my* end – shake
a little static

from your pj's fabric –
jumpstart
my paroxysmal heart

or plant a jolt
– tulip bulb, plumb bob –
into my not-as-hot

bod
I can pay, I've paid
all day – see here

I'm in ruins

* * *

* * *

* * *

Midnight Arrhythmia

1.

It's practical, I've read, to picture death.

To plan (with broken hands)

                        for those who go   into the fields we cannot sow—

      it's practical,   but still I have no will.

    Could I measure all   I'd owe

                   you both—postcards, HMOs, my love

                           expressed in shoveled snow—   and leave it here?

That's good—this sanding down   of splintered wood.

2.

My son, you gather   sticks & bark:

                      pistols, throttles   to dreamt-up cars & shuttles—

    the harvest of our evening walk.

           You blast me again and again.   I mime my most dramatic end

and wonder if you wonder

about a world in which we're mist   or less,

            in which we scatter

                     through brick & branch,   birdbath & mulch?

3.

A friend thinks it cruel   to teach you we go—calls it perverse.

That's naïve.

    Kids have always imagined worse,   notching

        their darker thoughts   into the fabric of their preschool cots.

    Sleep alone

    permits them—sweet   dissemblers, their parents' protectors—

        to dredge up demons.

    I watch the seismic shudder   of a nightmare you will not share

4.

and press your pitching hand   into my chest.

    Feel the tremor   that holds me

        here, but stay awhile—little starfish,

little ear—and it'll crest   in paroxysmal roar.

        This happens more and more—a tock-tick

        that tips to chronic.

My secret fear?   This heart is yours.

    With age, the docs say, *a-fib cascades.*   They also note, *it's all inborn.*

5.

Hot or cold: I get, I guess, to pick,

    which probe   to thread from crotch to chest

            and pass   (*oh yay*) into my broken heart.

      This part hurts most: I'm made cliché.

The hot's exact

    but can cause holes—like an eraser   rubbed too hard on paper.

The cold cannot, but it might shock   the phrenic nerve.

        Both recircuit (i.e. scar)   this mis-wired atrial wall.

6.

But if I linger longer

here—if I stall with your stuffed animals—

         then more of me   sneaks past

    the anesthetic's leaden pour.   My tactic's your unspoken adage:

filibuster what you can't manage.

Still, I know where I'm headed:

       ablate this fucking heart   before it's too late.

       Think reward, think risk.   If I don't wake up, you've still got this.

7.

How, you'd ask, *does a-fib feel?*

Like a flickering florescent bulb; like the dips in a country road.

And it hits like hiccups or divine indifference—

few episodes, in short, have an M.O.

Drink more, drink less; yoga Wednesdays, five deep breaths—

it's all pretense. Our bodies are less

you or *me* than leaves whipped into a T-storm.

I see mine trailing an I.V. like a kite string

8.

and dream of crimes I would commit

to keep you & your mom near: I'd torch our language's last book.

I'd flay endangered species on tenterhooks.

I'd warehouse summer. I'd Persephone each hour.

It doesn't help.

I imagine your mother stroking a future spouse's steadfast pulse

or you remaking me through story—

I'm a roll of iPhone photos & shitty, self-indulgent journals.

9.

Scuff on your sneakers after a walk;

the swish of the dishwasher while we three read books;

        the dog's claws clicking down the uncarpeted stairs;

    bedrooms cool, a curtain of air—

      that patchwork of weeds

      that brush us as we trudge to the bus stop;

          mice mazing round this 100-year-old brickwork;

and our days like bright ivy growing into the attic—

10.

dip me in *these*

moments before the incision—

      let the knife remind me of life's real crime:

      you can only record scant bits of it before you die.

    Or let's just revel

in one more lazy weekend—laundry festooned in rings, the *New York Times*,

      the languorous sway of our porch swing—

        tattoo those hours *here*. Let them sting.

11.

Ditto the bon mots & mottos,

   the lessons I would—decades hence—press on you.

         Can I pluck a few from future me

    and seed them now pre-surgery?

Take the bus when you can; fuck that line you'll hear (*be a man*);

Spurn comma splices   but not satisfying vices—

and when some old dude opines about the past, *question him*—

          especially if he's your dad.

12.

But—leave something more

  than what your namesake saw outdoors: the afterlife as lawn.

      In other words, *will* some scrap of self to live on.

  A patent, garden, kids, or poem— you pick.

  But steel yourself against its loss,

which'll probe your peripheral vision— like a smoke detector's

         red button or that bat

   I caught in a recycling bin. That's one I left: my big, homeowner win.

13.

Improv, I think, is just like life.

We move to cues— the only plan, *yes, and?*

because *yes, no* would be the end of the show—

    the dust motes drift; the curtain grows old.

    Last year I watched

        some revelers—their limbs gave in to purest play—

as they crept, leapt, & listened to my colleague's lyrical direction:

    "Let gold crowns lift you off the ground" and they rise

14.

weightless as the sky.

I wish that I were inhibition-less, trusting

    enough—one guy crumbles like "a statue in surf"—

    to fall or fail. Instead I fear

I've taught you to fear risk (one more parental whiff).

    I watch them mimic drunks, get stuck to boards, or hoard

    one intoxicating posture.

    I watch them—my god—learn: the only wrong answer

15.

is inaction.

Is that the trick—to see   all gifts (wife, kid)

       as evanescent   bliss; to know   imagination is all

                             we can control;   and to play right through

our use-by date?

      (A young man, his jaguar prowl   now done, gnaws a Clif Bar.)

                             Shall we bid adieu to delays?

                             Shall I end this dithering   that keeps the cardiologist at bay?

16.

Small son—here comes your tiger & your pig.

They paw your arm

                     and climb the amber light of your alarm.   I leave this room

    to them   and dreams.

     Maybe heaven isn't real, you mused   today as I tied our shoes,

                               but it should include endless hallways with endless books.

May yours lift up   from the floor

                     then land upon your bed like tents.

17.

A possum paws the fence.

The compost shrugs its rinds and pits.

Branches whisk   the moonlight pooling in the bowls of my glasses.

         Your mother's ankle   pins me to the mattress.

An ambulance's caterwaul

             dopplers   down the road; a window

                   splashes red, resets—   it's evening.

                           Life passes into pages if it passes into anything.

18.

Love, do you still count sheep?

I now count shelves,   a tapestry

         of selves (not souls)   that any finger might release.

             You know they've got spines too—   that's right, they do.

Let's peek inside

the oldest we can find   and—feel its uneven edge?—knife

                   the final pages free.

              Can you hear it,   like a patient, whisper: *thank god you opened me.*

For the Gods Now Gathering Over Omaha, Nebraska

We made you   because we needed someone to talk to.

We kept you   to give cursing more flair.

       If perched still on some hardscrabble hillside,   if bearded in our nightly despair—

              remember:

                      this Honda outruns a prayer.

See the temple at the end

       of this highway's bright tendril?

             See its high-poled antennas poke holes in your clouds?

    Its mosaics   and interfaith pamphlets

                 bring believers together   like a murder of crows.

O Gods, O.G.s of the Abrahamic squad,

       how long I've shunned your songs   only to find you sharing quarters.

  If one building's big enough

              to hold you all   should we suppose you're shrunken?

                        Is this expansion or rebranding?

                                            ❦

                This air seethes   with the cicadas' static;

                  These fields   are hopscotched with soybean & wheat.

Windows down, alone

                        with my body's sounds, I envy   anyone

                                          who is convinced you all are listening—

who does not feel   in a sunburn's peel

       this pride: I know that I will end.

                                              I am blessed with a beginning.

The Fog at Leadbetter Point State Park

Oysterville, Washington

Born of nowhere
& everywhere
a woolen reunion
between these dunes
& the clouds

we walk from it
but within it
dissolving into
its cold carbonation
like sugar like light

terminus of this earth
or its embryo
a silvery eureka
or indecision recast
as a wet film

I don't know
but we evanesce
in slow succession
like one two three
windows lit by rain

how does one ghost
cloak a coastline
& will our laughter
carry us forward
like a harness of bells

I can already tell
I'll be the first to look
backward first
to see our footprints
trail off like a fuse

hoary oasis
gossamer closet
you won't unspool
till I'm alone
in surf and in wind

as in a tireless
conversation
my body bending
like a trail post
back into the trees

Gegenschein

Oregon Museum of Science and Industry

1.

Lewis & Clark are dead.

And whoever marked time by the spin of a Jupiter moon: they're dead and gone to bloom.

    And their grandkids died by lightbulb.

The night, I've read, shone clear   at the 19th century's start, but cities

    marred that darkness.

My son tells me to ignore the stars.

He tries out a line I taught him: *once a cookie hits the floor it's just a dirty cookie.*

    This was all at OMSI, its halls bestrewn

with crumbs and kids galore, their post-snack bodies   oddly still before a globe

that spins up through the eons.

    Its continents split like chips of ice—

    Papa, how long's the world been breaking?

The question, love, is moot.

Today we ask: how long's it been our problem?

2.

I'm a sucker for outdated tropes.

Waterfalls and moss-sheathed woods are still, for me, Edenic.   I walk past them

        to lose the sun

                these explorers followed westward.   And then I see its glow residual—

rays passed through gas & dust—that dressed their eastern evening.

Gegenschein, it's called:

the idyll's dark reflection.

        Once, three hours west of here, we saw   a tree

that marks the spot where Clark first saw the Pacific.

                We biked up to its trunk and photographed our child   beneath its shadow.

The tree is bronze, the real one's gone.

                                    My son clanged it like a gong

        to call back all those clear-cut.

Thank god for kids.   Kids don't loathe the species they're extending.

3.

I dreamt last night of the Bering Strait,

its land bridge thinning like Play-Doh pulled from either end,

        the last family crossing before it sloughs off   into the Arctic.

        I saw Adam, Eve, and all their kin

                      trekking south toward Cali's Central Valley.

The years slip by; the family multiplies.

They hold a backyard party.

        Eve roasts a hog she'd just named   while the kids take turns telling stories.

            The night is full of love & beer

        until a grandkid clamors up Adam's knee   and asks about this New World

spread like a buffet before him.

It's okay, he shrugs, a little drunk, *but nothing's as good as Eden.*

The Cloud

I am the expanse in which everyone meets, repository

of bodies that never share air on the street.

Can you feel the dust tingle in a room you're left in alone?

Hear the whir of my viscid zeros and ones? I am a tomb.

I've held your kids in photos, emails, and vids—all this

because someone sold you a tale: the cloud never fails.

I am here to make your past clear as a pasture

after rain, bright as the touchscreen concealing your pain.

Moons wane, trucks brake, pop music still sounds fake—

but look: you rise through the flue of my uploads.

One day they'll find you beneath keystrokes of new fallen snow.

Exhausted Renegade Elephant

Blunder of tonnage, passable trampling—

    the elephant, of course, is never   to blame.

Most catastrophes today involve handler malfeasance:

    whole systems asleep   at the proverbial wheel, the wheel

turned toward ease or profit.

    And so it seems with Tiny, tranquil now

at the squad cars' clumsy roadblock,   victim of a smoke-break swap in shifts

    (Barb in pachys, flirty; Bob in monkeys, horny)

that leaves a corn dog cart crushed.   Some folks fume, some blame the zoo,

    until the footage proves that Bob did all his jobs.

⁕

Which brings me to my child,

    blacked out in the back seat of our car, stricken with *something*—

moldy peaches? norovirus?—that'll cost him

    three of thirty pounds. We try to keep his fluids down,   but don't succeed

till the anti-emetics and I.V.   Our doctor's face is a placid lake we stare into and sigh.

I could share

            our fears of failed parental care   or the relief

when he returns to dancing on the couch,

        but the inexplicable scared us more than sickness—   the causeless calamity

that ate up a day.   *Did you say day?*—my wife corrects.

       Two weeks we lost learning how thin a thin kid can get—

and two hours Tiny spent uncaged.   She crashed through brambles, rambled galumphing

        until a smattering of sirens

caused her to pause.   Here she is snoring like a semi in rain.

                  ❧

       And we who've an impulse to account for all carnage—

could we sing with the entropists   who embrace chaos as pure?

       We have, thank god, our tired metaphors:

the perfect storm, the act of god, and this elephant   asleep on my son's floor,

        a plush toy he carried from the hospital to bed.

He'll tug its ears, hug it hard,   then punch it in the head.

In the Land Between Sex and Conception

there are no trees, save
the shadows of trees, and words

that roll their shadows to root.
Whatever line will divide

the earth from the sky
hasn't yet squinted its sight

down the globe. The wind lulls
in translucent coils

and unrolls to release all the birds.
The beasts nest in their own

thought balloons. And you—
unborn notion, no skin

yet to float on—do you lounge
here in oceans still learning

to pool? Or are you dispersed
like so many concertgoers

awaiting the music's faint cry?
It will come, it will come

to where the rivers now run
like dreams in the grooves of a knife.

The Dead Cooper's Hawk

(a juvenile)

Feathered eyelids sealed
tight till I—it's easy
as fingering corduroy—

reveal two vacant,
yellow eyes. Who knew
accipiters blink up?

My brother. He'll bag
raptor bodies, hide
them whole in freezers.

I flip a drained
rain barrel & splay
the hawk across the top:

blood flecks necklace
his chest, a throat
gouged like a second

voided mouth.
Can any species die
of an outsized cry?

When I unfurl
a scythe-like talon
& pull its curled keratin

along my wrist,
the tip skips
like a turntable needle

or my brother's latest
howl: *We're nothing
but fucking animals.*

Once he'd taught me
that Cooper's eyes
redden as they get older—

as if hardship brims
from wingtip to crest
till they blink crimson.

The dead bird's blade
draws out a bead
of blood, its final cut.

The moon rises
slowly as the ring left
by a wet tin cup.

I could, he'd muse,
press harder. I could—
but I'd just grow colder.

Ode to Aphaea

Aegina, Greece – 2018

*   *   *

*   *   *

*   *   *

Huntress hunted
by lusty Minos
deity that Wiki deems

worthy
of minor entry
– boy, do we dudes owe you –

you who leapt
from cliff to fishing net
– gropes to ropes –

whom Artemis
rescued then wrapped
in deathlessness,

you've got a view
– of prows, of crowds –
a temple too,

but – oops at the voting
booth – we kinged
the one you duped –

So let us atone
with more
than stone

or shiny tickets,
proof – yes – of mere
admission

Let us lift you
over Wifi, Euros, fro-yo –
let us sing you

in and after
season – flip-flops, dreamin' –
till you rise up

again – untouchable –
a geyser
in the Aegean

* * *

* * *

* * *

For the Last Human

Once you knew others, at least   a mother.

How *does* ego change   when the other *Is* are all smothered?

    Selfishness precedes you into extinction,

        though it's selfishness that led you   like a guide dog

            toward this unholy distinction.

You're easy to conjure   in times of despair

and easier   to envy—you're free to not care.

    We see you sway gently   in a cobweb of words;

        our old borders   dissolved like vaporous clouds.

You own every inch

        of the footprints   you leave in the snow.

    Could we wander   like you wander—a firefly

    adrift above seas?   Are you like a magnet lodged in a tree?

                        You teach us   how little we control

                        Do you make us wiser?   We simply feel old.

Your end in the end   will come before dawn:

the sun's just a sun—   your shadow alone will know   that you're gone.

The Period at the End of This Sentence

    is larger than the lounge window

       where a waiter stacks the last barstool

and larger than the smile   of your child as he tells his first joke.

         It's larger than the stars   at play on the pond's face

    when the snow geese flee south.

It holds

all craters, equators, meteors, & our moon.

              It folds up   the *We're Closed* sign that hangs from a doorknob

        in space as the last   trace of matter

                  swirls down a drainpipe   of gravitational waste.

So goes the "closed theory"   of everything's end.

Blue shift moving—   heaven hits send.

And what'll become of our likeness? Your shyness? This sky?

    And how will light—shimmer of flecked silver—

unstick from the cosmos's eye?

        Will it land like a fly on God's placemat and expand?

        Will it burst like a snowball hurled at a screen?

∽

If so our wintry sequel and dream

      is smaller than the love

           in a protester's eye when she sees her friend standing

   after the tear gas has died.

It's smaller than the sink of beard hair & lather my dad cleaned.

Here's the moonlight;

there's your mother— this ending is smaller

     than both put together.

       Here's the idea that grips you as we read about physics:

our world will contract to the head of a pin; we'll all be sucked in.

Fuck quasars, fuck black holes—

Fuck the shuttle's proud flame—   *your* response is astounding:

Hey, our beginning and end are the same.

NOTES

"The Ghost Ship"

"In 1849 [...] the inhabitants of Yerba Buena saw hundreds of ships drop anchor in the bay; their crews simply abandoned everything, cargo and all, and headed for the hills to look for gold." The ships would later be "dismantled and used as landfill for streets." *San Francisco* (Knopf Guides, 1993).

This poem is for Ann Townsend.

"The Journal of Glacial Archaeology"

This poem takes its title from a peer-reviewed academic journal.

"A Poem for the Scoundrel Lucian Freud"

Geordie Greig's *Breakfast with Lucian: The Astounding Life and Outrageous Times of Britain's Great Modern Painter* (Farrar, Straus and Giroux, 2013) was essential in the writing of this poem.

Additional sources include Martin Gayford's *Man with a Blue Scarf: On Sitting for a Portrait by Lucian Freud* (Thames & Hudson, 2013); Robert Hughes's *Lucian Freud: Paintings* (Thames & Hudson, 1989); and David Stabler's article on *Three Studies of Lucian Freud* in *The Oregonian* (December 16, 2013). The novel quoted in section nine is James Salter's *A Sport and a Pastime* (Doubleday, 1967).

Three Studies of Lucian Freud was on view at the Portland Art Museum from December 2013 to March 2014. It sold at Christie's for $142.4 million. The buyer, initially anonymous, has since been identified as Elaine P. Wynn.

"Odes to Asklepios"

These poems are for Bronwen Wickkiser.

"Midnight Arrhythmia"

1.4   "I have no will": a lapse that has since been corrected.

5.1-8   Ablation procedures continue to evolve, as does their glossary of terms. The two methods mentioned here are radio frequency ablation (RF) and cryo-ablation (CB), which risk cardiac tamponade and phrenic nerve palsy (PNP), respectively.

12.2   "the afterlife as lawn": his namesake is Walt Whitman.

13.7   "my colleague's lyrical direction": I'm indebted to Heidi Winters Vogel for a job talk that became the basis for this scene.

17.8   "*Life passes into pages if it passes into anything*": James Salter's memoir, *Burning the Days* (Random House, 1997). With thanks to Adrianne Frech, who sent me a signed copy.

"For the Gods Now Gathering Over Omaha, Nebraska"

This poem responds to the 2015 building of the Tri-Faith Initiative on the banks of Hell Creek.

"Gegenschein"

This poem is for David Baker.

"Exhausted Renegade Elephant"

This poem was inspired by Joel Sternfeld's photograph, "Exhausted Renegade Elephant, Woodland, Washington, 1979," at the Portland Art Museum.

ACKNOWLEDGEMENTS

Action, Spectacle: "Midnight Arrhythmia"; *Always Crashing:* "The Reality Television Star," "The Cloud," and "For the Last Human"; *American Literary Review:* "In the Land Between Sex and Conception"; *Arion:* "Odes to Asklepios," "Ode to Aphaea," and "Partially Restored Statue of a Silver Bull"; *At Length:* "A Poem for the Scoundrel Lucian Freud"; *Booth:* "The Journal of Glacial Archaeology"; *Free Inquiry:* "For the Gods Now Gathering Over Omaha, Nebraska"; the *Kenyon Review:* "When the Earth Flies into the Sun"; *New England Review:* "Exhausted Renegade Elephant"; *Northwest Review:* "The Period at the End of This Sentence"; *Ocean State Review:* "The Ghost Ship"; *Pleiades:* "Gegenschein"; *Potomac Review:* "How to Keep Yourself Awake"; *Tusculum Review:* "A Poem for the 21st Century"; and *Zócalo Public Square:* "To the First Speaker."

Thank you Wabash College and its Byron K. Trippet Research Fund, which supported the writing of this book. Thank you Wabash College and its Coss Faculty Development Fund, which supported the use of Bacon's *Three Studies of Lucian Freud* on the cover. Thank you Robin Vuchnich for designing that cover. Thank you David Baker, Jonathan Farmer, Charles Kell, D.A. Powell, & Connie Voisine. Thank you Christopher Kempf. Thank you Marianne Chan, T.R. Hummer, Randall Mann, & Brian Turner. Thank you Henry Israeli, Rebecca Lauren, Timothy Liu, Sarah Wetzel, & everyone at Saturnalia Books. Thank you Willapa Bay Artist-in-Residence program.

Thank you Robert, Jean, and Ryan Mong. Thank you Chris Brandon (1955-2023). Thank you Cameron Guenther, who inspired "When the Earth Flies into the Sun." Thank you Bronwen Wickkiser, who invited me to join her and her students on two immersion trips to Greece.

Derek Mong is the author of two previous poetry collections from Saturnalia Books—*Other Romes* and *The Identity Thief*—and a chapbook, *The Ego and the Empiricist*, from Two Sylvias Press. His poems, essays, and translations have appeared widely: the *LA Times*, the *Boston Globe*, the *Kenyon Review*, *Pleiades*, *Free Inquiry*, and the *New England Review*. He and his wife, Anne O. Fisher, received the Cliff Becker Translation Award for *The Joyous Science: Selected Poems of Maxin Amelin* (White Pine Press). Together they run the literary journal, *At Length*. A contributing editor at *Zócalo Public Square*, he lives with his family in Indiana where he chairs the English Department at Wabash College.

Also by Derek Mong

Other Romes

The Identity Thief

The Ego and the Empiricist

When the Earth Flies into the Sun was printed in Adobe Garamond
www.saturnaliabooks.org